THE PROCESSIONS

Published by
Black Pinnacle LLC
www.blackpinnacle.com

English language translation copyright © 2015
Ghassan Maroun Kassab
Maroun Ghassan Kassab
Fady Ghassan Kassab

First published in the United States of America by Black Pinnacle LLC

ISBN-13: 978-0692366059 (Black Pinnacle LLC)

ISBN-10: 0692366059

Illustrations:
Original illustrations by Gibran Khalil Gibran are in the public domain in the United States of America.
New reproductions of the illustrations are copyright of Black Pinnacle LLC, 2015

Gibran Khalil Gibran

THE PROCESSIONS

Translated by

Ghassan M. Kassab

With
Maroun G. Kassab & Fady G. Kassab

Contents

Introduction

In 1919, Gibran Khalil Gibran published his Arabic masterpiece of poetry, "The Processions". The book was published at his own expense. He personally illustrated the book and took great care in the selection of the paper stock and even the font. This was not only a labour of love and stunning mastery of the Arabic language; albeit showing little regard to the classical school of Arabic poetry, but also a great insight into Gibran's view of the world.

Gibran had come to the United States from very humble beginnings, from the mountains of Lebanon and the village of Bcharri, and had become an acclaimed author, poet and painter. Bcharri is a town that rests its head in the snowy mountains of the Cedars of Lebanon and extends its feet to reach the sacred "Valley of the Saints" (Wadi Kadisha). It was there, in 1883, where Gibran Khalil Gibran was born. In the Valley of the Saints villages spread alongside a river which runs to the sea, separating the mountains and leaving a large green canopy of trees and flowers. This marvellous canopy surrounds old stone houses that still stand there today, defying time. Images of Gibran's homeland echo throughout the poem and much of his life's joys and sufferings are mirrored in its lines.

At twelve years of age, after the short imprisonment of his father for embezzlement and the family teetering on the brink of destitution, he immigrated with his mother and three siblings to the United States, where he studied art and began his literary career, writing in both English and Arabic. In the Arab world, Gibran is regarded as a rebel, with confronting literary and political views. He had a very unique romantic style that was at the heart of a renaissance in modern Arabic literature, especially prose poetry, breaking away from the classical Arabic school.

In Lebanon, he is celebrated as a literary hero and just short of a deity. He is primarily known in the English-speaking world for his 1923 book "The Prophet", an early example of inspirational fiction that contains a series of philosophical essays written in poetic English prose.

Gibran's contemporary, the Syrian-born poet and writer Nasib Arida wrote an introduction to "The Processions" that many later took to be Gibran's intention in the poem.

"Before reading this book, let the reader imagine a large meadow at the foot of a mountain. There, by chance, two men meet. One is old and the other is a youth. The first had come out of the city and the second from the woods. The old man walks slowly, leaning on his cane with a shaking hand. His face and long grey hair carry the marks of one who had battled time and uncovered the secrets of life and tasted so much of its bitterness that he had become a pessimist. This old man arrives at the meadow and lies on the grass, seeking rest. Suddenly a youth with soft, sun-bronzed skin, filled with the joy and happiness of life, comes out of the woods carrying his reed.

He walks until he reaches the spot where the old man was resting and lies next to him. Barely a minute of silence passes before they start having a conversation. The old man starts telling his view on life as perceived through his pessimistic side and veteran experience. The young man replies, explaining life as seen through his jovial, optimistic eyes."

Gibran personally never mentions an old or a young man. He simply starts the poem with the words:

The good in men is wrought by force,

And vice in men outlasts their course,

And most of men are tools moved by

Fingers of time, one day, then die.

So do not say this man is smart,

Nor of that an aristocrat,

As best of men are herds that race

At shepherds' voice, or else, efface.

Whether the poem truly is a discussion between sage and youth or just the contrasting thoughts of a dreamy philosopher, "The Processions" remains one the most beautiful and complex philosophical works ever produced in the Arabic language. This book aims to provide the first complete and most accurate translation to date.

Translating poetry into poetry from one language to another is always a challenging task and in the case of Gibran's immortal poem, "The Processions", the challenge becomes colossal. We hope that this translation has captured the spirit and message of Gibran Khalil Gibran in an accurate and beautiful manner. It is an invitation to marvel at Gibran's poetic wisdom and genius.

The Processions

The good in men is wrought by force,

And vice in men outlasts their course,

And most of men are tools moved by

Fingers of time, one day, then die.

So do not say this man is smart,

Nor of that an aristocrat,

As best of men are herds that race

At shepherds' voice, or else, efface.

In the woods there is no shepherd,

No! Nor is there in it a herd!

Winter leads each year yet Spring

Has its very own song to sing!

Men are born slaves to obey

The one who says to yielding: Nay!

So if he is to rise one day

Marching, he will lead the way.

Give me the reed and sing away,

For singing tends the troubled mind,

And the sigh of the reed will stay,

Beyond despised and glorified.

Life's but a slumber, with dreams, at best,

Of he who heeds his soul's request,

For the spirit's secret is cloaked by sadness,

Or else it's cloaked by happiness,

And the secret of living is veiled by ease,

If lifted, vex will veil the scenes,

So if you can hold from ease and vex,

You'd near His shadow who's minds perplexed.

In the woods there are no tears,

No! Nor are there worries or fears,

If one day a calm breeze blows,

It brings no poison as it goes,

The spirit's grief is an illusion's ghost,

That does not last and soon is lost,

And through the clouds of the soul is seen,

The sight of stars plain in between.

Give me the reed and sing away,

For singing wipes away distress,

And the sigh of the reed will stay,

After Time desists, no less.

And few on earth accept their lives

As come, unfazed by boredom's guise,

So most transform life's river's flow

To cups that numb when gulped, and so

If people drink they gladly glow,

As pledged to love, sedated though,

One riots when prays, the other beams

If rich, another dwells on dreams!

For earth is a winery, its master: Time

Those drunk alone can accept its prime,

So if you see one sober, wonder loud:

Did the moon take shade by a rainy cloud?

In the woods, there is no intoxication,

Neither from wine nor imagination,

For in the streams you'll only find

The clouds' elixir left behind,

Drugging is but, in fact, a breast

And milk for weaklings, for their rest,

So when they die, after they age,

That's when they reach their weaning age.

Give me the reed and sing away,

For singing is the finest drink,

And the sigh of the reed will stay,

After hills fall down and shrink.

Religion in men is but a field,

Sawed by those who have a need,

One hoping for eternal life,

One dunce who fears the fire's strife,

If men feared not the Judgment Day,

Won't worship God or even pray,

As if their faith is just a trade:

Persist, thus win, neglect, thus fade.

In the woods you will not find

Religion or heresy of any kind,

For if the bulbul a song would sing,

Won't claim his song the rightful thing!

Men's religion will come and go,

But like a shadow, lasts not though,

On earth there's been no religion past

That of Taha and the Christ to last.

Give me the reed and sing away,

For singing is the best of prayers,

And the sigh of the reed will stay,

After life the death gown wears.

Justice on earth would cause jinn to cry

If heard of, and the dead to laugh so high,

For criminals, small, get prison hold;

High ranks get pride, glory and gold,

Who steals a flower is scorned and jailed,

Who steals a field is brave and hailed,

Who kills the body gets killed by deed,

Who kills the soul, no one would heed.

In the woods there is no justice,

No! Nor punishment or redress,

For if the willows cast their shade,

Upon the earth and on the glade,

The Cypress trees won't say or look,

At it as heresy against the book!

Justice in men resembles snow,

If seen by the sun will melt and thaw.

Give me the reed and sing away,

For singing is the justice of hearts,

And the sigh of the reed will stay,

After guilt ends and departs.

Might is right, and if souls are strong

They dominate; if weak they change along,

For the scent in the lion's den will scare

Jackals away, den full or bare,

And starlings are cowards, even in flight,

Yet falcons, in dying, have pride and might,

The soul's might is a right none can defy,

Whether men accept it or deny,

So if you see a weakling chief he'd be,

Upon those who'd from their reflections flee.

In the woods there is no might,

No! Nor is there weakness in sight,

If lions roar they don't proclaim

Their roar the fearsome thing to name!

For people's might is just a ghost,

Floating in the space of thought,

And people's rights will sure wear out,

Like leaves in autumn do, no doubt.

Give me the reed and sing away,

For singing is the might of souls,

And the sigh of the reed will stay,

Long after suns crumble and fall.

Knowledge in men has a starting date,

Its end is set by time and fate,

And the best of knowledge is a dream, if scored,

And shown to sleepers you'd be scorned,

If you find a dreamer alone but then,

Accused, cast off, despised by men,

He is the prophet, by the future cloaked,

From a nation that wears its yester-coat,

He lives in the world yet a stranger there,

He speaks out loud without a care,

He's the strong one, yet kindness shows,

He's way ahead, men far or close.

In the woods there is no knowledge,

Nor ignorance anywhere to acknowledge,

If the branches dance to right and left,

They don't claim it's a thing to respect,

All the knowledge that men can yield,

Is just like fog upon a field,

When the sun would spread its rays,

The fog will lift and end its days.

Give me the reed and sing away,

For singing is knowledge at its best,

And the sigh of the reed will stay,

After stars reach their final rest.

The free on earth builds from his trends,

Unknowingly, a prison for his ends,

If he gets free from mankind's hands,

He stays a slave to what he loves and fans,

He's ingenious, yet how hard he aims,

Though for the truth, stays false in claims,

He's free, but in his haste for all,

Though reaches glory, he'd still be small.

In the woods there is no free,

Nor a dispraised slave to see,

For glories are absurd and low,

Like bubbles on the surface flow,

If almond trees their blossoms shed,

Upon the weeds below they spread,

They do not the weeds disdain,

As mighty gods upon them reign.

Give me the reed and sing away,

For singing does in glory stand,

And the sigh of the reed will stay,

Beyond the low life and the grand.

Gentleness in men is like a shell,

Though ribs are soft, no pearls do dwell,

One hypocrite with two souls to show,

One made of rock and one of dough,

Another thoughtless, soft in breed,

His clothes, like thorns, could make him bleed,

One scoundrel who shields in gentleness,

If he's afraid, or dangers press,

So if you find one gentle, yet with might,

Then you've found light for eyes' lost sight.

In the woods you'll find no gentle hand,

As mild as a coward in his stand,

For the branches of ben trees tower by,

Next to the oak trees, as tall and high,

And if peacocks were given feathers so draped,

Like a flowing, royal, purple cape,

They wouldn't know what this gift meant,

Whether it's beauty or ravishment!

Give me the reed and sing away,

For singing is the grace of the meek,

And the sigh of the reed will stay,

Beyond both, strong or weak.

Wryness is a disguise whose worst,

Are those who in its art are versed,

One fond of matters that he knows not,

No loss or gain from which he got,

One arrogant who thinks himself a king,

In all his words his greatness rings,

One haughty whose mirror has become his sphere,

His reflection a moon that beams so clear.

In the woods, you'll find no wry,

Whose wryness is so weak and dry,

For though sometimes the wind blows weak,

Its weakness doesn't sickness wreak!

Though rivers have flavors that truly are,

Exactly like that of nectar,

Yet in their hearts lies power and might

That sweeps large boulders without a fight.

Give me the reed and sing away,

For singing is the wryness' sign,

And the sigh of the reed will stay,

Beyond those dense or very fine.

Love comes in forms, most with no root,

Like weeds in fields, no flowers or fruit,

And a little of love, like wine sips, please,

But for the addict only gulps appease,

And if love is led by flesh's fire,

It suicides in a bed of desire,

Like a captive king betrayed by friends,

Refusing life, accepting ends.

In the woods you'll find no rake,

Claiming noble love for his sake,

If bulls would sometimes moo so loud,

They do not call it love's sweet sound!

For people's love is illness, shown

Clearly within the flesh and bone,

When youth will end, for good, my dear,

That illness too will disappear.

Give me the reed and sing away,

For singing is true love and grace,

And the sigh of the reed will stay,

Beyond a fair or a pretty face.

If you find a lover, in his love extreme,

Disdaining hunger, content with dreams,

Yet people say: what's this fool's gain

Or aim from love to carry that pain?

For this girl's love he bleeds his eyes!

And in her, no worth or beauty lies!

Say all are fools, before birth they died,

And never knew what sparks life inside.

In the woods there's none to blame,

Nor a guard to watch one's aim,

If the deer would restless get,

As the sun sets in the West,

Eagles won't say Alas! or rage,

Or even see it as something strange,

For when wisdom is not within our range,

We call him strange whose mind is sage.

Give me the reed and sing away,

For singing is the best of madness,

And the sigh of the reed will stay,

Beyond prudence and calmness.

We may forget invaders' pride,

Yet remember fools till seas Earth hide,

In Alexander's heart a massacre raged,

In Kaise's heart, a temple prayed,

In victories of the first a defeat was veiled,

In the latter's defeat victory prevailed,

For love is in the soul, not in the flesh, expressed,

Like wine is for inspiration, not drunkenness, pressed.

In the woods there's no mention there,

Except of lovers and their care;

For those who committed all sorts of things,

Invaded, oppressed and ruled as kings,

Ended just letters in books, the same

As in criminal lists, title and name,

For love disclosed is known secure,

Simply to us: Victory for sure!

Give me the reed, and sing away,

Forget the injustice of the strong,

Lilies, cups for dew are they,

Not for blood and acts of wrong.

Happiness in life is a pursued ghost,

When materialized, then that thrill is lost,

Like a river that hurls towards the plains,

Once there, slows down, muddies and wanes,

Pleasure is only in the quest,

To attain what's banned and then there's rest,

If you find one glad, and doesn't care

For power, say, his mind is fair.

In the woods you'll find no hope,

Nor any boredom with which to cope,

Why should the woods hope for a part,

When it has all within its heart?

In search of hope one seeks the woods,

For it has hope and all its goods,

Living in the woods is the hope to fulfill,

And living in hope is just another ill.

Give me the reed and sing away,

For singing is both light and fire,

And the sigh of the reed can a wish convey,

That can't be reached by a weak desire.

The purpose of the soul is concealed within,

And appearances can't show what hides therein,

Some say when souls perfection near,

Fade out and then they disappear,

As though they're fruits, once ripe, the trees

Would let them go for a passing breeze,

And others claim when bodies sleep,

There's nothing left for the soul to keep,

As though the soul is a shadow in a lake,

If water stirs all shadows break,

All have strayed, atoms don't perish

In bodies, nor in the souls are cherished,

For though North winds force herds to hide,

When East winds blow, their tails spread wide.

In the woods I found no distinction

Between body and soul to question,

For air is water swaying slow,

And dew is water without a flow,

And scents are flowers that roam at will,

And earth is flowers standing still,

And poplars shadows are poplars who,

Thought night had come and slept anew.

Give me the reed and sing away,

For singing is both body and soul,

And the sigh of the reed will stay,

Better than any drink at all.

Soul's home: the body, its peaceful womb,

When the soul matures and lofts, is doomed,

The soul's the embryo, and death its labour date,

Though no miscarriage or hardships await,

Yet men have ghosts that bind their wings,

Sterile, like bows not tied with strings,

Those are intruders, for souls are not

Born from dry trees, slime or dust,

For how many plants maintain no scent,

And how many clouds no rain have sent?

In the woods you will not find,

Sterile or intruder of any kind,

Within the date you find a seed,

That keeps the secret of the breed,

And in the honeycomb a story dwells,

Of bee hives and of fields and hills,

Sterile is just a word to utter,

Idleness forming its every letter.

Give me the reed and sing away,

For singing is a body that flowed,

And the sigh of the reed will stay,

Beyond all hybrids and deformed.

For sons-of-earth, death ends their quest,

For the ethereal, it's start and conquest,

Who longs for light in his dreams survives,

Who sleeps all night, by day he dies,

Who hugs the dust when he's awake,

Hugs dust till Venus' lights shall break,

Death is like the sea; could be crossed if light,

And who carries weights will drown outright.

In the woods you will not find,

Death or graves of any kind,

When April leaves the stage each year,

Joy still goes on, with all its cheer,

The fear of death causes confusion

In our hearts, like a delusion,

For living a single spring is like

Living for ages, all alike.

Give me the reed and sing away,

For singing is the secret of eternal age,

And the sigh of the reed will stay,

After existence folds its page.

Give me the reed and sing away,

Forget what you and I had said,

Speech is like dust, can't speak or say,

Just tell me what you really did

Did you take the woods as home, like me,

Instead of a castle with a golden dome?

Or followed the path of streams so free,

And climbed the rocks on hills you roam?

Have you once with perfume bathed,

And dried yourself with rays of light?

And sipped the dawn like wine dispensed

In ether cups that are so bright?

Did you, like me, at dawn, take rest,

In laps of vineyards and skies so clear,

Where bunches of grapes look their best,

Like glittering, golden chandeliers?

For thirsty souls, a spring they are,

And food for those with hunger quest,

They are honey, perfume and more by far,

And wine they are at one's request.

Did you, on grass, take one night's sleep,

And had the skies as cover too,

Renouncing what might come and heap,

Forgetful of what passed, in true?

The stillness of the night is a roaring sea

Whose waves are pounding in your ear?

And in the night a heart can be

heard pulsing in your sleep to hear?

Give me the reed and sing away,

Forget both illness and the cure,

For people: Lines of verse are they,

Yet scribed with water, alas, for sure.

I wish I knew what good comes out

Of meetings and gathering in a crowd,

And of debates and all that shout,

Of these disputes, heard out so loud!

Tunnels of moles they are in strife,

And a spider's web with all its breadth,

If one with difficulty lives his life,

His life is just one long, slow death.

Living in the woods, if the days, I said,

Were in my hands, in the woods I'd spread,

But Time with me has aims and needs,

Whenever I seek the woods it pleads,

Destiny's ways will never change,

And weaklings' aims fall short in range.

❖

❖

العيشُ في الغاب و الأيام لو نُظمت

في قبضتي لغدت في الغاب تنتشر

لكن هو الدهرُ في نفسي له أَربٌ

فكلما رمتُ غاباً قامَ يعتذرُ

و للتقادير سبلٌ لا تغيرها

و الناس في عجزهم عن قصدهم قصروا

اعطني الناي و غنِّ

و انسَ دأءًا و دواء

انما الناس سطورٌ

كتبت لكن بماء

ليت شعري اي نفعٍ

في اجتماع و زحامْ

و جدالٍ و ضجيجٍ

و احتجاجٍ و خصامْ

كلها انفاق خُلدٍ

و خيوط العنكبوتْ

فالذي يحيا بعجزٍ

فهو في بطءٍ يموتْ

هل فرشتَ العشب ليلاً

و تلحفتَ الفضا

زاهداً في ما سيأْتي

ناسياً ما قد مضى

و سكوت الليل بحرٌ

موجهُ في مسمعكْ

و بصدر الليل قلبٌ

خافقٌ في مضجعكْ

هل جلست العصر مثلي

بين جفنات العنبْ

و العناقيد تدلتْ

كثريات الذهبْ

فهي للصادي عيونٌ

و لمن جاع الطعامْ

و هي شهدٌ و هي عطرٌ

و لمن شاءَ المدامْ

اعطني الناي و غنِّ

وانس ما قلتُ و قلتا

انما النطقُ هباءٌ

فأفدني ما فعلتا

هل تخذتَ الغاب مثلي

منزلاً دون القصورْ

فتتبعتَ السواقي

و تسلقتَ الصخورْ

هل تحممتَ بعطرٍ

و تنشفت بنورْ

و شربت الفجر خمراً

في كؤُوس من اثيرْ

ليس في الغابات موتٌ

لا و لا فيها القبور

فاذا نيسان ولّى

لم يمتْ معهُ السرورْ

إنَّ هول الموت وهمٌ

ينثني طيَّ الصدورْ

فالذي عاش ربيعاً

كالذي عاش الدهورْ

اعطني الناي و غنِّ

فالغنا سرُّ الخلود

و أنين الناي يبقى

بعد ان يفنى الوجود

و الموتُ في الأرض لابن الارض خاتمةٌ

و للأثيريّ فهو البدءُ و الظفرُ

فمن يعانق في احلامهِ سحراً

يبقى و من نامَ كل الليل يندثرُ

و من يلازمُ ترباً حالَ يقظتهِ

يعانقُ التربَ حتى تخمد الزهرُ

فالموتُ كالبحر ، مَنْ خفّت عناصره

يجتازه ، و أخو الاثقال ينحدرُ

ليس في الغابِ عقيمٌ

لا و لا فيها الدخيلْ

إنَّ في التمر نواةً

حفظت سرّ النخيلْ

و بقرص الشهد رمزٌ

عن قفير و حقولْ

انما العاقرُ لفظ

صيغ من معنى الخمولْ

اعطني الناي و غنِّ

فالغنا جسمٌ يسيلْ

و أنينُ الناي ابقى

من مسوخ و نغولْ

و الجسمُ للروح رحمٌ تستكنُّ بِهِ

حتى البلوغِ فتستعلى و ينغمرُ

فهي الجنينُ و ما يوم الحمام سوى

عهدِ المخاض فلا سقطٌ و لا عسرُ

لكن في الناس اشباحاً يلازمها

عقمُ القسيِّ التي ما شدَّها وترُ

فهي الدخيلةُ و الأرواح ما وُلدت

من القفيل و لم يحبل بها المدرُ

و كم عَلَى الارض من نبتٍ بلا أرجٍ

و كم علا الافقَ غيمٌ ما به مطرُ

لم اجدْ في الغابِ فرقاً

بين نفس و جسدْ

فالهوا ماءٌ تهادى

و الندى ماءٌ ركدْ

و الشذا زهرٌ تمادى

و الثرى زهرٌ جمدْ

و ظلالُ الحورِ حورٌ

ظنَّ ليلاً فرقدْ

اعطني النايَ و غنِّ

فالغنا جسمٌ وروح

و أنينُ الناي ابقى

من غبوق و صبوحْ

و غايةُ الروح طيَّ الروح قد خفيتْ

فلا المظاهرُ تبديها و لا الصوَرُ

فذا يقول هي الأرواح إن بلغتْ

حدَّ الكمال تلاشت و انقضى الخبرُ

كأنّما هي أثمار إذا نضجتْ

و مرَّتِ الريح يوماً عافها الشجرُ

و ذا يقول هي الأجسام ان هجعت

لم يبقَ في الروح تهويمٌ و لا سمرُ

كأنّما هي ظلٌّ في الغدير اذا

تعكر الماءُ ولّت وامّحى الاثرُ

ضلَّ الجميع فلا الذرّاتُ في جسدٍ

تُثوى و لا هي في الارواح تختضرُ

فما طوتْ شمألُ اذيال عاقلةٍ

الّا و مرَّ بها الشرقيْ فتنتشرُ

ليس في الغابِ رجاءٌ

لا و لا فيه المللْ

كيف يرجو الغاب جزءًا

و عَلىَ الكل حصلْ

و بما السعيُ بغابٍ

أملاً و هو الأملْ

انما العيش رجاءًا

إحدى هاتيك العللْ

اعطني النايَ و غنِّ

فالغنا نارٌ و نورْ

و أنين الناي شوقٌ

لايدانيهِ الفتور

و ما السعادة في الدنيا سوى شبحٍ

يُرجى فإن صارَ جسماً ملهُ البشرُ

كالنهر يركض نحو السهل مكتدحاً

حتى اذا جاءَهُ يبطي و يعتكرُ

لم يسعد الناسُ الا في تشوُّقهمْ

الى المنيع فان صاروا بهِ فتروا

فإن لقيتَ سعيداً و هو منصرفٌ

عن المنيع فقل في خُلقهِ العبرُ

ليس في الغابات ذكرٌ

غير ذكر العاشقينْ

فالأولى سادوا و مادوا

و طغوا بالعالمين

اصبحوا مثل حروفٍ

في أسامي المجرمينْ

فالهوى الفضّاح يدعى

عندنا الفتح المبينْ

اعطني الناي و غنِّ

و انس ظلم الأقوياء

انما الزنبق كأسٌ

للندى لا للدماء

66

و قل نسينا فخارَ الفاتحينَ و ما
ننسى المجانين حتى يغمر الغمرُ

قد كان في قلب ذي القرنين مجزرةٌ
و في حشاشةِ قيسٍ هيكلٌ وقرُ

ففي انتصارات هذا غلبةٌ خفيتْ
و في انكساراتِ هذا الفوزُ و الظفرُ

و الحبُّ في الروح لا في الجسم نعرفهُ
كالخمر للوحي لا للسكر ينعصرُ

ليس في الغابات عذلٌ

لا و لا فيها الرقيبْ

فاذا الغزلانُ جُنّتْ

اذ ترى وجه المغيبْ

لا يقولُ النسرُ واهاً

ان ذا شيءٌ عجيبْ

إنما العاقل يدعى

عندنا الأمر الغريبْ

اعطني الناي و غنِّ

فالغنا خيرُ الجنون

و أنين الناي ابقى

من حصيفٍ و رصينْ

68

فان لقيتَ محباً هائماً كلفاً

في جوعهِ شبعٌ في وِردهِ الصدرُ

و الناسُ قالوا هوَ المجنونُ ماذا عسى

يبغي من الحبِّ او يرجو فيصطبرُ

أفي هوى تلك يستدمي محاجرهُ

و ليس في تلك ما يحلو و يعتبرُ

فقلْ همُ البهمُ ماتوا قبل ما وُلدوا

أنّى درواكنهَ من يحيي و ما اختبروا

ليس في الغابِ خليعٌ

يدَّعي نُبلَ الغرامْ

فاذا الثيران خارتْ

لم تقلْ هذا الهيامْ

انَّ حبَّ الناس داءٌ

بين حلمٍ و عظامْ

فاذا ولَّى شبابٌ

يختفي ذاك السقامْ

اعطني النايَ و غنِّ

فالغنا حبٌّ صحيحْ

و أنينُ الناي ابقى

من جميل و مليحْ

70

و الحبُّ في الناس أشكالٌ و أكثرها

كالعشب في الحقل لا زهرٌ و لا ثمرُ

و أكثرُ الحبِّ مثلُ الراح ايسرُه

يُرضي و أكثرهُ للمدمنِ الخطرُ

و الحبُّ ان قادتِ الاجسامُ موكبهُ

الى فراش من الاغراض ينتحرُ

كأنهُ ملكٌ في الاسر معتقلٌ

يأبى الحياة و أعوان له غدروا

ليس في الغابِ ظريف

ظرفهُ ضعف الضئيلْ

فالصبا و هي عليل

ما بها سقمُ العليلْ

انّ بالانهار طعماً

مثل طعم السلسبيلْ

و بها هولٌ و عزمٌ

يجرفُ الصلدَ الثقيلْ

اعطني الناي و غنِّ

فالغنا ظرفُ الظريفْ

و أنين الناي ابقىٰ

من رقيق و كثيفْ

و الظرفُ في الناس تمويةٌ و أبغضهُ

ظرفُ الأولى في فنون الاقتدا مهروا

من مُعجبٍ بأمورٍ و هو يَجهلها

و ليس فيها له نفعٌ و لا ضررُ

و من عتيٍّ يرى في نفسهِ ملكاً

في صوتِها نغمٌ في لفظها سُوَرُ

و من شموخٍ غدت مرآتهُ فلكاً

و ظلهُ قمراً يزهو و يزدهرُ

73

ليس في الغابِ لطيفٌ

لينهُ لين الجبانْ

فغصونُ البان تعلو

في جوار السنديانْ

و اذا الطاووسُ أُعطي

حلةً كالارجوانْ

فهوَ لا يدري أحسنٌ

فيهِ ام فيهِ افتتان

اعطني الناي و غنِّ

فالغنا لطفُ الوديعْ

و أنين الناي ابقى

من ضعيفٍ و ضليعْ

و اللطفُ في الناسِ اصداف و إن نعمتْ

أضلاعها لم تكن في جوفها الدررُ

فمن خبيثٍ له نفسان واحدةٌ

من العجين و أُخرى دونها الحجرُ

و من خفيفٍ و من مستأنث خنثٍ

تكادُ تُدمي ثنايا ثوبهِ الإبرُ

و اللطفُ للنذلِ درعٌ يستجيرُ بهِ

ان راعهُ وجلٌ او هالهُ الخطرُ

فان لقيتَ قوياً ليناً فبهِ

لأَعينٍ فقدتْ ابصارها البصرُ

ليس في الغابات حرٌّ

لا و لا العبد الذميمْ

انما الأمجادُ سخفٌ

وفقاقيعٌ تعومْ

فاذا ما اللوز القى

زهره فوق الهشيمْ

لم يقلْ هذا حقيرٌ

و انا المولى الكريمْ

اعطني الناي و غنِّ

فالغنا مجدٌ اثيلْ

و أنين الناي ابقى

من زنيمٍ و جليلْ

و الحرُّ في الأرض يبني من منازعهِ

سجناً لهُ و هو لا يدري فيؤتسرُ

فان تحرَّر من ابناءٍ بجدتهِ

يظلُّ عبداً لمن يهوى و يفتكرُ

فهو الاريب و لكن في تصلبهِ

حتى و للحقِّ بُطلٌ بل هو البطرُ

و هو الطليقُ و لكن في تسرُّعهِ

حتى الى اوجِ مجدٍ خالدٍ صِغرُ

ليس في الغابات علمٌ

لا و لا فيها الجهولْ

فاذا الأغصانُ مالتْ

لم تقل هذا الجليلْ

انَّ علمَ الناس طُرَّا

كضبابٍ في الحقولْ

فاذا الشمس اطلتْ

من ورا الافقِ يزولْ

اعطني النايَ و غنِّ

فالغنا خير العلومْ

و أنينُ الناي يبقى

بعد أن تطفى النجومْ

و العلمُ في الناسِ سبلٌ بانَ أوَّلُها

امَّا اواخرها فالدهرُ و القدرُ

و أفضلُ العلم حلمٌ ان ظفرت بهِ

و سرتَ ما بين ابناء الكرى سخروا

فان رأيتَ اخا الاحلام منفرداً

عن قومهِ و هو منبوذٌ و محتقرُ

فهو النبيُّ و بُرد الغد يحجبهُ

عن أُمةٍ بِرداءِ الأمس تأتزرُ

و هو الغريبُ عن الدنيا و ساكنها

و هو المهاجرُ لامَ الناس او عذروا

و هو الشديد و إن ابدى ملاينةً

و هو البعيدُ تداني الناس ام هجروا

ليس في الغابات عزمٌ

لا و لا فيها الضعيفْ

فاذا ما الأُسدُ صاحت

لم تقلْ هذا المخيفْ

انَّ عزم الناس ظلٌّ

في فضا الفكر يطوفْ

و حقوق الناس تبلى

مثل اوراق الخريفْ

اعطني الناي و غنِّ

فالغنا عزمُ النفوسْ

و أنينُ الناي يبقى

بعد أن تفنى الشموسْ

و الحقُّ للعزمِ و الارواح ان قويتْ

سادتْ و إن ضعفتْ حلت بها الغيرُ

ففي العرينة ريحٌ ليس يقربهُ

بنو الثعالبِ غابَ الأسدُ أم حضروا

و في الزرازير جُبن و هي طائرة

و في البزاةِ شموخٌ و هي تختضر

و العزمُ في الروحِ حقٌ ليس ينكره

عزمُ السواعد شاءَ الناسُ ام نكروا

فإن رأيتَ ضعيفاً سائداً فعلى

قومٍ اذا ما رأَوا اشباههم نفروا

ليس في الغابات عدلٌ

لا و لا فيها العقابْ

فاذا الصفصاف ألقى

ظله فوق الترابْ

لا يقول السروُ هذي

بدعةٌ ضد الكتابْ

انَّ عدلَ الناسِ ثلجُ

إنْ رأتهُ الشمس ذابْ

اعطني الناي و غنِ

فالغنا عدلُ القلوبْ

و أنين الناي يبقى

بعد أن تفنى الذنوبْ

و العدلُ في الأرضِ يُبكي الجنَّ لو سمعوا

بهِ و يستضحكُ الاموات لو نظروا

فالسجنُ و الموتُ للجانين إن صغروا

و المجدُ و الفخرُ و الإثراءُ إن كبروا

فسارقُ الزهر مذمومٌ و محتقرٌ

و سارق الحقل يُدعى الباسلُ الخطر

و قاتلُ الجسمِ مقتولٌ بفعلتهِ

و قاتلُ الروحِ لا تدري بهِ البشرُ

ليس في الغابات دينٌ

لا و لا الكفر القبيحْ

فاذا البلبل غنّى

لم يقلْ هذا الصحيحْ

إنَّ دين الناس يأْتي

مثل ظلٍّ و يروحْ

لم يقم في الأرض دينٌ

بعد طه و المسيح

اعطني الناي و غنِّ

فالغنا خيرُ الصلاة

و أنينُ الناي يبقى

بعد ان تفنى الحياةْ

و الدين في الناسِ حقلٌ ليس يزرعهُ

غيرُ الأولى لهمُ في زرعهِ وطُرُ

من آملٍ بنعيمِ الخلدِ مبتشرٍ

و من جهول يخافُ النارَ تستعرُ

فالقومُ لولا عقاب البعثِ ما عبدوا

رباً و لولا الثوابُ المرتجى كفروا

كأنما الدينُ ضربٌ من متاجرهمْ

إن واظبوا ربحوا او اهملوا خسروا

ليس في الغابات سكرٌ

من مدامٍ او خيالْ

فالسواقي ليس فيها

غير اكسير الغمامْ

انما التخديرُ ثديٌ

و حليبٌ للانامْ

فاذا شاخوا و ماتوا

بلغوا سن الفطامْ

اعطني النايَ و غنِّ

فالغنا خير الشرابْ

و أنين الناي يبقى

بعد أن تفنى الهضاب

و قلَّ في الأرض مَن يرضى الحياة كما

تأتيهِ عفواً و لم يُحكم بهِ الضجرُ

لذاك قد حوَّلوا نهر الحياة الى

أكوابٍ وهمٍ اذا طافوا بها خدروا

فالناس ان شربوا سُرّوا كأنهم

رهنُ الهوى و عَلىَ التخدير قد فُطروا

فذا يُعربدُ ان صلَّى و ذاك اذا

اثرى و ذلك بالاحلام يختمرُ

فالأرض خمارةٌ و الدهر صاحبها

و ليس يرضى بها غير الألى سكروا

فإن رأَيت أخا صحوٍ فقلْ عجباً

هل استظلَّ بغيمٍ ممطرٍ قمرُ

ليس في الغابات حزنٌ

لا و لا فيها الهمومْ

فإذا هبّ نسيمٌ

لم تجىءْ معه السمومْ

ليس حزن النفس الاَّ

ظلُّ وهمٍ لا يدومْ

و غيوم النفس تبدو

من ثناياها النجومْ

أعطني الناي و غنِّ

فالغنا يمحو المحنْ

و أنين الناي يبقى

بعد أن يفنى الزمنْ

و ما الحياةُ سوى نومٍ تراوده

احلامُ من بمرادِ النفس يأتمرُ

و السرُّ في النفس حزن النفس يسترهُ

فإن تولىَّ فبالأفراحِ يستترُ

و السرُّ في العيشِ رغدُ العيشِ يحجبهُ

فإن أُزيل توَّلى حجبهُ الكدرُ

فإن ترفعتَ عن رغدٍ و عن كدرِ

جاورتَ ظلَّ الذي حارت بهِ الفكرُ

ليس في الغابات راعٍ

لا و لا فيها القطيعْ

فالشتا يمشي و لكن

لا يُجاريهِ الربيعْ

خُلقَ الناس عبيداً

للذي يأبى الخضوعْ

فإذا ما هبَّ يوماً

سائراً سار الجميعْ

أعطني النايَ و غنِّ

فالغنا يرعى العقولْ

و أنينُ الناي أبقى

من مجيدٍ و ذليلْ

الخير في الناس مصنوعٌ اذا جُبروا

و الشرُّ في الناس لا يفنى و إِن قبروا

و أكثر الناس آلاتٌ تحركها

أصابع الدهر يوماً ثم تنكسرُ

فلا تقولنَّ هذا عالم علمٌ

و لا تقولنَّ ذاك السيد الوَقرُ

فأفضل الناس قطعانٌ يسير بها

صوت الرعاة و من لم يمشِ يندثر

المواكب

جبران خليل جبران

الخيرُ في الناس مصنوعٌ اذا جُبروا

و الشرُّ في الناس لا يفنى و إِن قبروا

و أكثرُ الناس آلاتٌ تحركها

أصابعُ الدهر يوماً ثم تنكسرُ

فلا تقولنَّ هذا عالمٌ علمٌ

و لا تقولنَّ ذاك السيد الوَقِرُ

فأفضلُ الناس قطعانٌ يسير بها

صوتُ الرعاة و من لم يمشِ يندثر

المواكب

جبران خليل جبران

www.ingramcontent.com/pod-product-compliance
Lightning Source LLC
Chambersburg PA
CBHW081339090426
42737CB00017B/3209